Ferrari

FERRARI ALBUM **1**

Ferrari

FERRARI ALBUM 1

Edited by Jonathan Thompson

 **The Color Market**

Editor/Designer   Jonathan Thompson
Publisher   Donald H. Dethlefsen
Typography   Central Graphics, San Diego, California
Color Separations   Color Masters, Phoenix, Arizona
Printing   The Color Market, Northbrook, Illinois

for Beverly

Published by **The Color Market**, 3000 Dundee Road, Suite 201,
        Northbrook, Illinois 60062

ISBN 0-940014-01-7

Printed in the United States of America

CONTENTS

Four-Fives
Ferrari 375 MM Berlinettas and Spyders 6

126 C
Ferrari's first supercharged car since 1950 28

Ghia
bodywork on Ferrari chassis 36

Bob Tronolone Portfolio:
Front-engine Ferrari sports cars in California races 44

BB 512 LM, 308 GTB/4 Turbo and 365 GTB/4 run at
Daytona 1981 56

Ferrari auf dem
Nürburgring 58

Acknowledgements 96

Four-Fives
Ferrari 375 MM Berlinettas and Spyders

THE FERRARI 375 SERIES—in fact, several groups of cars with an almost undefinable range of detail variations—was the most important "type" employing the big single-overhead-camshaft V-12 engines developed by engineer Aurelio Lampredi in the early 1950s. The designation 375, from Ferrari's single-cylinder capacity numbering system, works out to exactly 4500 cc when multiplied by 12, although there were two different bore/stroke configurations, 80 x 74.5 mm giving 4493.73 cc, and 84 x 68 giving 4522.08, while the type number was also used for the big 4.9-liter, the 375 Plus (84 x 74.5 mm, 4954.34 cc).

For both Formula 1 and sports car racing, the 375s grew out of 275 (3.3-liter) and then 340 (4.1) engines. This increase was made very quickly during 1950 for the Grand Prix cars, for which the unsupercharged capacity limit was 4.5 liters. We are concerned here with the 375 Mille Miglia series of competition sports cars, comprising some twenty-eight machines with serial numbers between 0318 AM and 0512 AM, built with Pinin Farina berlinetta and spyder and Vignale spyder carrozzeria. They were used by the factory as well as private owners for races in Europe, Africa, and North and South America, mainly during 1953-54, with varying degrees of success.

Lampredi had worked for Società Anonima Piaggio & C., an aeronautical firm which weathered the immediate post-World War 2 period of recovery by concentrating on the production of Vespa motor scooters. He also worked at Isotta-Fraschini on its last project, the stillborn rear-engine Monterosa V-8. He joined Ferrari in 1949 at the age of twenty-two, as an assistant to Ing. Gioacchino Colombo, designer of the original series of Ferrari V-12 engines from the 125 S through the 250 GT, developed further by other engineers. Lampredi lacked a university degree in engineering but learned well from his practical experience. It was his idea to abandon the two-stage supercharged 1.5-liter Colombo Formula 1 engine and to build an unsupercharged 4.5 unit which, lacking the absolute power potential of the smaller blown engine, could come close on peak output while gaining great advantages in torque and reduced fuel consumption, the latter saving much time on pit stops. This was the strategy for beating the Alfa Romeo 158, itself a Colombo design from just before the war and still dominating Grand Prix racing in 1950. It took Lampredi and Ferrari little over a year to be proved right.

The first unsupercharged Ferrari Formula 1 car, the 275 F1, made its debut in the Belgian Grand Prix at Spa-Francorchamps on June 18, two months after the first appearance of the 275 S sports car in the Mille Miglia. Driven by Alberto Ascari, the 275 F1 had dimensions of 72 x 68 mm, giving a displacement of 3322.34 cc and an output of 280 bhp at 7000 rpm, not enough to compete with the Alfas but sufficient for a 5th-place finish. Six weeks later a 320-bhp 340 F1 engine was available for Ascari to use in the Grand Prix des Nations at Geneva, and for the important Italian Grand Prix at Monza in September there were two full 375 F1 cars with 330 bhp. By early 1951 power was up to 350 bhp and Froilan Gonzalez' famous victory in the British Grand Prix at Silverstone, followed by Ascari's wins at the Nürburgring and Monza, proved Lampredi's point. So much so that Alfa Romeo retired from racing after a fortunate victory at Barcelona and the 1952-53 seasons were relegated to Formula 2 competition

375 engine designer Aurelio Lampredi, right, with 1952-53 World Champion driver Alberto Ascari.

Luigi Villoresi at the wheel of the 375 F1 at Reims in 1951.

Lampredi watches as Meazza adjusts the carburetion on the 375 F1 at the Nürburgring before the 1951 German Grand Prix.

because there was no suitable competition for the big Ferraris.

Lampredi designed an extremely effective twin-overhead-cam four-cylinder engine which dominated Formula 2, while the V-12s were further developed for sports car events. The transition from 275 to 375 in this category took a full three years, with the 4.1-liter 340 America, MM and Mexico cars forming Ferrari's principal effort during 1951-52. The debut of the 4.5-liter 375 MM (using an F1-derived 4494-cc engine as distinct from the later, customers' 375 MM which displaced 4522 cc) came in the Le Mans 24-hour race in June 1953, in one of three 340 MM chassis with Pinin Farina berlinetta bodywork. This car, 0318 AM, was reputed to have the 1952 Indianapolis version of the Grand Prix 4.5; at any rate it had magneto ignition and connecting rods machined from steel billets rather than forged, and its output was probably close to 350 bhp for Le Mans if not anything like the 400 bhp claimed for the Indianapolis unit. Driven by Ascari and Luigi Villoresi, it was a rabbit which set a lap record of 181.642 km/h (112.8 mph) but suffered clutch trouble and was finally retired after ten hours. After Le Mans the 375 MM berlinetta ran in the Reims 12-hour race, driven by Umberto Maglioli/Piero Carini; it set a lap record but was disqualified for a push-start.

In mid-July the other two 340 MM berlinettas (0320 AM and 0322 AM, now owned by Bob Sutherland and Ernie Beutler respectively) were brought up to 375 capacity and all three were given new noses, slightly more streamlined with lower radiator intakes and flush plastic headlight covers; the curved rear windows were replaced by flat glass surrounded by sheet aluminum. Altogether these were about as brutal-looking as a Fifties closed car could be. The factory assembly sheets for these cars show a majority of 340 components, with 375-type engine internals, as well as those carrying the early 275-based part numbers. The lesson is that any Ferrari engine can have (and during this period probably did have) whatever components were considered suitable, or simply available, for a particular purpose. In mid-1953 the purpose was further racing and the factory campaigned the cars at Spa, Senigallia and Pescara during July and August before they were shipped off, along with 0358 AM (built from the start as a 375 MM) for Umberto Maglioli, to Mexico and the fourth running of the Carrera Panamericana.

At Spa there were no cars capable of threatening the Ferraris on performance, but the 24 Heures de Francorchamps was a long race; Ascari/Villoresi again lost a clutch, Maglioli/Carini lost a valve, and the winning car of Mike Hawthorn and Nino Farina, the only 375 MM to last, was making ominous rear-axle noises as it reached the finish. At Senigallia Hans Ruesch got ahead of the 4.5s at the start with his Touring-bodied 340 MM spyder; Villoresi's 375 MM spyder Vignale (with 4522-cc engine) passed him on the second lap, only to suffer piston failure on lap 5. Paolo Marzotto's 375 MM berlinetta passed Ruesch the next time around and went on to win the race at an average speed of 159.758 km/h (99.2 mph). The third successive victory for the type came in the 12 Ore di Pescara, where Hawthorn and Maglioli were the winners at 128.551 km/h (79.8 mph) after team manager Nello Ugolini wisely reduced the pair's speed, which had included a lap at 144.385 km/h early in the race. The second 375 MM berlinetta of Villoresi/Marzotto retired, after having led for several hours, with the characteristic malady, rear-axle failure.

At the end of August the 375 MM spyder Vignale, probably the one used by Villoresi at Senigallia, won the ADAC 1000-km Rennen at the Nürburgring after the Lancias encountered electrical trouble. Driven by Ascari and Farina, the car had a variation on the familiar, stubby series of Vignale spyder bodies which had been seen on 166, 250 and 340 MM chassis, perhaps starting out as one of the latter. It was distinguishable by external headlights with bezels; the following year it was used by Phil Hill in the final Carrera Panamericana, painted white and sporting a somewhat ridiculous tailfin. A 375 MM berlinetta had also been entered for the German race but its engine was borrowed when the spyder's broke in practice, leaving Hawthorn and Villoresi without a drive.

The three "low-nose" 375 MM berlinettas went to Mexico as Scuderia Guastala entries for Mancini/Salviati, Stagnoli/Scotuzzi and Cornacchia/Ricci. The first "true" 375 MM was the berlinetta of Maglioli/Cassini; although similar in general proportions to its 250/340/375 MM forerunners, the Pinin Farina body differed in many details, including a nose and semi-recessed hood scoop like those that would be seen on Farina's 375 MM spyders early in 1954, as well as slightly bulged rear fenders improving upon the sheet-metal scoops which had been added for tire clearance on the earlier cars. This body style was a limited-production design

Gerino Gerini drove this 4.5-liter berlinetta, similar to the 1953 Le Mans car, in the 1954 Mille Miglia. Note low exhaust!

The 4.5-liter 340/375 MM berlinetta of Ascari/Villoresi at Le Mans in 1953; it set a lap record but retired after 10 hours.

The 375 engine used at Le Mans had the Formula 1 dimensions of 80 x 74.5 mm, giving 4494 cc and approximately 350 bhp.

The two 375 MM berlinettas at Pescara in 1953; the Villoresi/Marzotto car (6) leads that of winners Maglioli/Hawthorn here.

(probably nine cars) built with a variety of details according to customers' needs, ranging from fairly stark competition form to road-car finish with small bumpers, chromium side trim and even two-tone paint. But Maglioli's car was an all-out racing machine, with external hood latches, low-mounted brake scoops and possibly, as some enthusiasts have speculated, a 4.9-liter engine, then under development for the 375 Plus which would appear officially in 1954. It was certainly fast, the only Ferrari able to challenge the Lancia D24s until Maglioli lost a wheel at over 200 km/h. He took Cornacchia's place in the Ricci 4.5 berlinetta, but its low position at that point meant that he was only classified 6th at Juarez, despite winning the last three stages. The berlinetta of Mancini/Salviati finished 4th overall, assuring Ferrari of the 1953 sports car championship, but that of Stagnoli/Scotuzzi (0318 AM) crashed on the second stage, with fatal results for both driver and co-driver.

Engine of Nürburgring Vignale spyder was the first true 375 MM with 84 x 68-mm bore and stroke, giving capacity of 4522 cc.

Seen before the start of the 1953 Nürburgring 1000-km race, the 375 MM spyder of Ascari/Farina had typical Vignale lines.

Phil Hill and Richie Ginther cross the finish line at Juarez to place the 375 MM spyder 2nd in the 1954 Carrera Panamericana.

Repainted but still with headrest and tailfin, the 375 MM Vignale spyder won Torrey Pines in 1955, driven by Shelby.

First of the limited-production Pinin Farina 375 MM berlinettas had redesigned bodywork; this is 0358 AM, Maglioli's Mexico car.

Maglioli drove 0358 AM in the 1953 Carrera before losing a wheel and switching to Carini's older car to finish the race.

The Rubirosa/Baggio 375 MM berlinetta before the start of the 1954 Le Mans race; the car (0380 AM) was shown at Geneva earlier.

While identical in basic contours, the Pinin Farina 375 MM berlinettas differed in many small details; note the "road" appearance of the two-tone example with bumpers and the competition character of Sebastiani's berlinetta, 0416 AM.

Roberto Bonomi's berlinetta in the 1954 Buenos Aires 1000-km race.

Dick Irish drove a spirited race on a damp track to place the Christensen 375 MM berlinetta 4th at Watkins Glen in 1954.

The last of Pinin Farina's 375 MM berlinettas, 0490 AM shown at Torino in 1954, suggested future 250 GT berlinetta styling.

The remaining "low-nose" 375 MMs (0320 AM and 0322 AM) passed through the hands of a number of American owners. The latter was raced several times in 1954 by Dick Irish while it was owned by M. P. Christensen. Irish was 4th at Watkins Glen in September after besting Walt Hansgen's Jaguar XK-120C and almost catching Sherwood Johnston's Cunningham C4R; he drove the same car (often referred to, incorrectly, as a "Mexico" because of its race there) at March Air Force Base in November, finishing 7th. Interestingly, the March AFB program gave its displacement as 4522 cc, which would mean the 84 x 68-mm dimensions of the customers' series 375 MM.

Farina designed a competition spyder body for this series, supplementing the limited-production berlinettas. The spyder shared most styling features with the closed car, although the front fenders curved downward on their way back to the open cockpit, making the rear fenders also stand out more prominently. There were visible rivets on the nose in front of the hood, a slight bulge on the rear deck for the fuel filler, and various combinations of windscreen, tonneau, auxiliary driving lights, brake scoops and even small bumpers.

It would appear from Farina's records and others' that fourteen of these spyders were built,

Pinin Farina 375 MM spyders had lines similar to those on berlinettas; again, each individual car was slightly different.

15

Three 375s and a 340 Mexico before the start of the 1954 Buenos Aires race; number 10 is the winning Farina/Maglioli spyder, 12 the converted 375 F1 of Rosier/Trintignant, and the next car is the 375 MM spyder of Ibanez/Janices.

When Saenz Valiente switched to a 4.9-liter 375 Plus, Carlos Najurieta bought his 375 MM spyder and raced it in 1955.

Piero Scotti's 375 MM spyder in the 1955 Mille Miglia; it was outclassed by the 6-cylinder cars, not to mention Moss's 300 SLR!

not counting the 375 Plus cars which were basically similar. But Farina's numbers don't always conform to the bodywork known to be on the particular chassis, leading to speculation whether they were rebodied by Farina or simply mis-identified in the original records. Among these were the two extremely interesting one-off coupes built for film director Roberto Rossellini: 0402 AM and 0456 AM. The former, listed in Farina records as a 375 MM spyder for Luigi Chinetti in 1954, was rebuilt in 1955 with an absolutely magnificent Scaglietti coupe body combining the basic lines of the 410 Sport (it may have been hammered over the same pattern) with a very small roof owing more than a little inspiration to the Mercedes-Benz 300 SL. The other special, 0456 AM, is listed among the Pinin Farina 375 MM berlinetta series but was built to a unique Farina design featuring a low, wide nose with retracting headlights, concave side sculpturing of the same general shape used later on the 1956 Corvette, and twin roof sails which were a bit capricious in 1954 but previewed a concept that would be fully developed on the Dino 206/246 GT, 308 GTB and Berlinetta Boxer, as well as numerous other PF show cars. The third road car using a competition-numbered chassis was 0488 AM, a cabriolet built for King Leopold of Belgium on a 375 MM base (listed by Farina within the berlinetta series), while 0490 AM was the last of the 375 MM berlinettas, specially dressed up by Pinin Farina for the 1954 Torino show, with tail fins, bumpers, and large air outlets on the sides of the fenders.

With the 375 MM no longer just a hot-rodded 340 but now a catalogued type with two styles of available *carrozzeria*, it is appropriate to examine its basic specification. As mentioned, the 4522-cc engine was used in the customers' series; this was a 60-degree V-12 with chain-driven single overhead camshafts, one for each bank of cylinders, operating two inclined overhead valves per cylin-

Extremely graceful coupe body was built by Scaglietti over 375 MM spyder chassis (0402 AM) in 1955. Contours are similar to 410 Sport.

Another Rossellini car, intended for Ingrid Bergman, was this unique Pinin Farina 375 MM coupe (0456 AM) shown at Paris in 1954. Fender recess may have inspired 1956 Corvette.

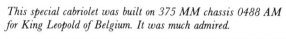

This special cabriolet was built on 375 MM chassis 0488 AM for King Leopold of Belgium. It was much admired.

der by roller cam followers and rocker arms, and hairpin valve springs. Ignition, with one spark plug per cylinder, was by two magnetos, mounted nearly vertically at the back of each camshaft. The compression ratio was 9.0:1 and three four-choke downdraft 40 IF/4C or 42 DCZ carburetors were used; power was quoted as 340 bhp at 7000 rpm. The clutch was of multiple dry plate type and the gearbox, mounted behind the engine, was a four-speed and reverse with synchromesh on all forward gears. The rear axle was live with limited-slip differential; available final-drive ratios were 7/31 (4.43), 8/32 (4.00), 9/32 (3.56) or 9/31 (3.44:1), giving maximum speeds at 7000 rpm in 4th gear, with 7.00 x 16 tires, of 224 km/h (139 mph), 248 (154), 279 (173) and 289 (179) respectively.

The frame was of large-diameter, elliptical-section welded steel tubing. Front suspension was by upper and lower A-arms, transverse leaf spring, anti-roll bar and Houdaille hydraulic lever-action shock absorbers. The rear axle was located by parallel trailing arms on each side, semi-elliptic leaf springs and Houdaille shock

---

375 MM

1 *Vignale spyder with 4522-cc engine. Serial number not known; probably converted from 340 MM.*

3 *Pinin Farina berlinettas with 4394-cc engines. Converted from 340 MM. Serial numbers 0318 AM, 0320 AM and 0322 AM.*

8 *Pinin Farina customer berlinettas with 4522-cc engines. Serial numbers 0358 AM (Cornacchia), 0368 AM (Cavallier), 0378 AM (Way), 0380 AM (Geneva 1954), 0416 AM (Sebastiani), 0456 AM (Rossellini, Paris 1954), 0472 AM (Ducato), 0490 AM (Torino 1954).*

14 *Pinin Farina customer spyders with 4522-cc engines. Serial numbers 0360 AM (Scotti, De Oliveira), 0362 AM (Factory, Gregory?), 0364 AM (Kimberly), 0366 AM (unknown), 0370 AM (unknown), 0372 AM (Cunningham?), 0374 AM (Parravano), 0376 AM (Rossellini), 0382 AM (Spear), 0384 AM (unknown), 0400 AM (Cunningham, liquid-cooled brakes), 0402 AM (Chinetti, converted to coupe by Scaglietti for Rossellini), 0450 AM (Bao Dai), 0460 AM (Day).*

1 *Pinin Farina cabriolet for King Leopold of Belgium. 4522-cc engine. Serial number 0488 AM.*

1 *Body type not known; probably Pinin Farina berlinetta. 4522-cc engine. Serial number 0512 AM.*

---

28 cars

---

absorbers. Brakes were hydraulic, two-leading-shoe type with finned aluminum drums. The wheelbase was 2600 mm (102.3 inches), the track 1325 (52.2) front and 1320 (52.0) rear, and the tires were Pirelli, 6.00-16 front and 6.50 or 7.00-16 rear, mounted on 5.0 x 16-inch Borrani center-lock wire wheels. Fuel capacity was 180 liters (47.6 U.S. gallons). Weight, always a doubtful figure in early Ferrari specifications, was quoted as *circa* (approximately) 900 kg, or 1984 pounds.

The first racing appearance of the 375 MM spyder was on December 20, 1953, in the Casablanca 12-hour race. The semi-private entry was shared by Piero Scotti and Scuderia Ferrari driver Farina, who won without much opposition. In practice Casimiro de Oliveira crashed the similar car (0360 AM, according to Pinin Farina) which he was to have shared with Ascari. A month later the factory 375 MM spyder of Farina/Maglioli won the first of the 1954 championship events, the Buenos Aires 1000-km race in Argentina; two other 4.5-liter cars ran there, the customer 375 MM spyder of Ibanez/Janices rolling over in a spectacular but fortunately not fatal accident, and the unusual Grand Prix-based, Scaglietti-bodied 375 F1 of Louis Rosier and Maurice Trintignant finishing 7th.

On March 7 at Sénégal, Farina and Scotti ran two spyders, the latter being the winner, but from this point on the factory ceased to run any 4.5s, having already begun racing the 4.9-liter 375 Plus at Agadir the previous month. Scotti was 3rd there in his 375 MM and also won the Giro della Toscana on April 11. Both he and Paolo Marzotto crashed 375 MM spyders in the Mille Miglia on May 2; as the same fate befell the 4.9s of Farina and Maglioli it was not a good race for Ferrari (who had won the 1000-mile race every year since 1948, but were beaten by Ascari's Lancia in 1954).

De Oliveira won the Hedemora 9-hour race with a 375 MM spyder on May 23; Scotti was 2nd at Siracusa on October 10 and won the Castelfusano 6-hour race on the 31st, both with a 375 MM spyder. As both drivers have been linked to 0360 AM, one wonders whether the customers' cars were traded back and forth by the factory as they were serviced during the season.

Briggs Cunningham bought a 375 AM spyder (0400 AM) and ran it in standard form at Sebring in 1954 before converting it to a novel but insufficiently developed liquid-cooled drum brake system for the Le Mans race that year. The car had large round scoops added in front, between the hood and fenders, for the brake coolant radiators;

it also had a larger radiator intake, additional scoops and louvers, and received Cunningham's regular white and blue paint scheme. Phil Walters and John Fitch drove it at Le Mans, running as high as 6th, but the brakes were less effective than regular drums, let alone discs, the system put added strain on the engine, which lost power, and the car eventually retired with final-drive failure. The various Cunningham team drivers, including Briggs himself, raced it a few more times in the U.S. before the brake system was converted back (the other body changes remaining) and the car sold to Sherwood Johnston, who won with it at Ft. Pierce and Cumberland in 1955. Dabney Collins raced it for Temple Buell several times later that year and in 1956.

Enrique Diaz Saenz Valiente, one of Argentina's best sports car drivers, campaigned a 375 MM spyder in his homeland throughout 1954, before selling it to Carlos Najurieta and stepping up to a 375 Plus. Among Saenz Valiente's successes with the 4.5 were the Premio Invierno, the Premio Independencia and the Premio Primavera, all in Buenos Aires, and the Gran Premio Plata Club Quilmer. Najurieta/Ribera brought the car into 2nd place in the 1955 Buenos Aires 1000-km race, behind its former owner's new 4.9. Another

Briggs Cunningham bought a 375 MM spyder, converted it to liquid-cooled brakes and ran it unsuccessfully at Le Mans in 1954. Among the extensive instrumentation was a dash-mounted decelerometer.

After a few races for Cunningham in the U.S., 0400 AM was sold to Sherwood Johnston, who won several times with it in 1955.

At the start of the 1954 Le Mans race the Rubirosa/Baggio 375 MM berlinetta moves off ahead of the Cunningham spyder of Walters/Fitch.

4.5 raced in Argentina in 1955 was the 375 MM berlinetta of Roberto Bonomi. And before going into the racing accomplishments of the 375 MM spyders in North America (essentially a different kind of competition in which the type's brute acceleration was well adapted to the flat, feature-less airport circuits then in major use), mention should be made of one further performance by a 375 MM berlinetta, in the 1954 Le Mans 24-hour race. This machine (0380 AM, the Geneva Show car), driven by Porfirio Rubirosa and Count Baggio, is perhaps most famous for the amount of time it spent in the sandbank at Tertre Rouge, where Baggio planted it firmly after four hours.

Four-nines were the answer for the final Carrera Panamericana in 1954, Maglioli winning a long-deserved victory in a 375 Plus, but Phil Hill, partnered by Richie Ginther, brought the "old" Vignale-bodied spyder into a fine 2nd place and Chinetti/Shakespeare were 4th in the latter's standard Farina spyder.

The list of American drivers who ran 375 MM spyders during 1954 and 1955 reads like a Who's Who in the sport at that time: Jim Kimberly, Bill Spear, Phil Hill, Jack McAfee, Masten Gregory, Bob Drake, Phil Walters, Sherwood Johnston, Erwin Goldschmidt, Duncan Black, Dale Duncan, Carroll Shelby, Lou Brero, Tom Bamford, Dabney Collins, and even Ken Miles. The most consistent campaigners of the type were Kimberly and

Spear. Kimberly more or less put Ferrari on the map in U.S. competition, starting out with a 166 MM Barchetta and working his way up to a 121 LM by way of a 195 S berlinetta Touring, a 225 S spyder Vignale, a 340 MM spyder Vignale, a 375 MM spyder Pinin Farina and a 375 Plus. All of these cars carried his famous yellow number 5, backed up by the best racing organization money could buy. His 375 MM spyder (0364 AM) was unique in having its body made to special order, with fenders cut away behind the wheels front and rear. If Kimberly didn't win everything in sight, he came close in 1954, scoring victories in the SAC races at the MacDill, Hunter, Bergstrom, Chanute, Atterbury, Westover and Lockbourne Air Force Bases that year. In 1955 the 4.5 fell off its trailer on the way to Sebring; after being repaired (without the cut-away rear fenders) it ran in bare metal at Beverly, Massachusetts, finishing 2nd to Hill's 750 Monza. It was later raced by Rich Lyeth, with the addition of a headrest and tailfin.

Bill Spear was probably a better driver than Kimberly. His list of successes (in 0376 AM) included Andrews AFB, Thompson and March Field in 1954, and a 2nd to Kimberly at Hunter AFB. The March Field race saw one of the most impressive turnouts of 4.5s for any event; following Spear into 2nd place was Hill in the Mexican Road Race Vignale spyder (displacement given as 4587 cc in the race program), then Johnston in the

Jim Kimberly's 375 MM spyder, 0364 AM, had special fenders, cut away behind the wheels. It won many SAC air base races in 1954.

Damaged on the way to Sebring in 1955, Kimberly's 375 MM was repaired, without cutaway rear fenders, and raced unpainted at Beverly. Rich Lyeth later ran it with headrest and tailfin.

Bill Spear won several important events in his 375 MM spyder; here (number 1c) he passes Kimberly (5) to win the Andrews AFB race.

Tony Parravano holds the wheel of his 375 spyder before the 1955 Sebring race, in which it caught fire.

Masten Gregory, sharing his 375 MM spyder with Clemente Biondetti, took 4th in the 1954 Reims 12-hour race.

ex-Cunningham Pinin Farina spyder (converted back from its water-cooled brake configuration and painted blue), Kimberly in 6th place and Irish in 7th with the Christensen berlinetta.

Jack McAfee was one of several drivers to use Tony Parravano's 375 MM spyder (0374 AM), winning at Golden Gate Park and Offutt AFB in 1954. Bob Drake won with it at Palm Springs the same year. At Sebring in 1955 the car caught fire, the rear part being extensively burned before it was extinguished. At Bakersfield, McAfee flipped it.

Masten Gregory, one of the first Americans to make a significant impression in European events, ran his 375 MM in France and England before bringing it back to the U.S. Paired with Clemente Biondetti, Gregory took a 4th place in the Reims 12-hour race on July 4 and three weeks later he drove it to a good 3rd in the Grand Prix of Portugal, behind the 750 Monzas of Gonzalez and Hawthorn. He also ran at Goodwood (2nd) and Aintree (1st), and set the fastest time in the rainy Prescott hillclimb, before scoring a 2nd at Montlhéry and then his biggest success with the car, a 1st in the Nassau Trophy race in December.

Erwin Goldschmidt on his way up Giant's Despair in 1:01.26. He also won the Edenvale, Ontario race in this 375 MM spyder.

This color photo of a 375 MM spyder was used by Ferrari in a brochure giving the specifications of the projected 410 Superamerica. Similar to a photo used on a Road & Track *cover at the time, it depicts 0460 AM, the Day car which was never raced and exists in original condition today.*

No less than five 375 MMs ran in the 1954 March AFB race. Spear won in number 4, followed by Hill in the Vignale spyder (2c) and Johnston in the ex-Cunningham car (100); Kimberly (5) was 6th and Irish brought the berlinetta (115) in 7th.

26

Erwin Goldschmidt won the Giant's Despair hillclimb in his 375 MM spyder, setting a time of 1:01.26, and also won at Edenvale, Ontario, in Canada. At the end of 1954 it was his new 375 Plus that Maglioli used to win in Mexico. Duncan Black's 375 spyder took Giant's Despair in 1955, with a slightly slower time of 1:02.04 (Shelby would set a record of 0:58.768 with the NART 375 F1 in 1956).

At the NASCAR Speed Week at Daytona Beach in 1955, Jack Rutherford ran 153.724 mph in a 375 MM, compared to 170.538 for Boris Said in the 375 F1 and 154.823 for Kimberly's 375 Plus.

Shelby won the 1955 Torrey Pines event with the Vignale spyder driven by Hill in Mexico and at March AFB the previous Fall. From mid-1955 the 375 MM spyders continued to run in various U.S. events, but the type was no longer competitive, being outpaced by the 4.9s, the four-cylinder 750 Monzas and the six-cylinder 121 LMs. The last significant victory for a 375 MM spyder was by Shelby at Mansfield in March 1957.

Lampredi's 4.5-liter engine had achieved its goal in Formula 1 and performed effectively in sports car racing before being enlarged to 4.9 liters for the 375 Plus. This will be the subject of a forthcoming FERRARI ALBUM, along with the other 4.9s, the 410 Sport and Special.

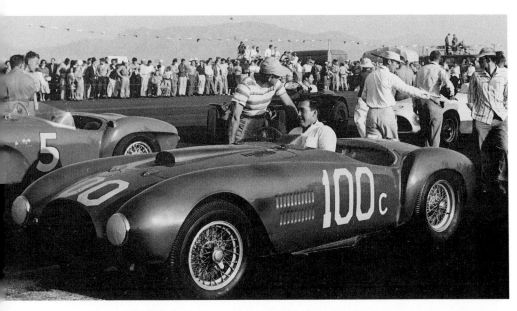

126 C

AFTER THIRTY YEARS, Ferrari has returned to the supercharger in Formula 1. In mid-1950, when the first of the big, normally-aspirated, 3.3, 4.1 and 4.5-liter Lampredi V-12s began to supplant the 1.5-liter supercharged Colombo engines, blower technology was left behind. During 1952-55 Ferrari used 2.0 and 2.5-liter four-cylinder inline engines, then Jano's 2.5 Lancia V-8 in 1956-57, the 2.5 Dino V-6 from 1958-60 and the 120-degree Dino V-6 in the 1.5-liter formula from 1961 through 1965, with a brief appearance by the first of the flat-12s. The Scuderia ran V-12s for the initial four years of the 3-liter formula, 1966-69, before embarking on the long boxer program that saw them score 37

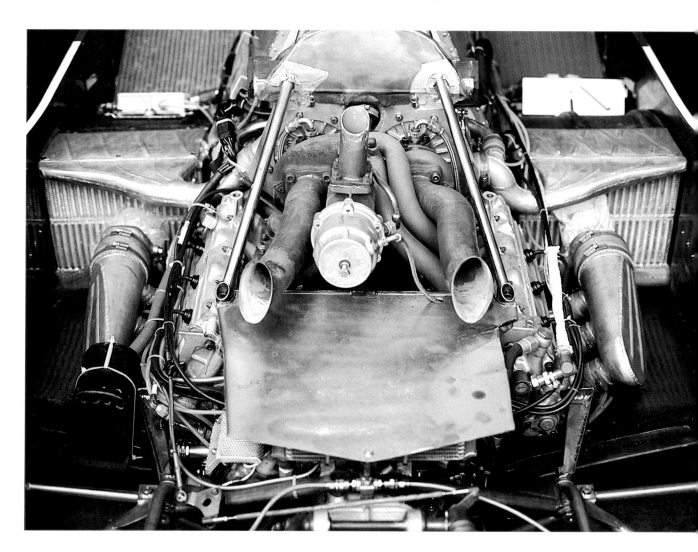

First Ferrari supercharged car was 125 F1, built in single-stage short-wheelbase form in 1948. In 1949 a long-wheelbase two-stage car ran at Monza in the Italian Grand Prix; this is Villoresi in the 1950 version of that machine.

victories, three drivers' and four constructors' titles with Forghieri's 3.0 flat-12 during 1970-80. The 1980 season was the first bad one for Ferrari in years, and the reason was not the boxer engine's ineffectiveness but rather the team's preoccupation with an entirely new kind of power plant, the turbo.

Impressed by the promise of Renault's V-6 turbo, even if it has not yet shown an *overwhelming* superiority, Ing. Mauro Forghieri began studies for the boxer's replacement as early as 1977 and started serious design work the following year. By that time, another reason for a new engine had made itself clear: the development of

Left, the KKK-turbocharged V-6 engine as mounted in Gilles Villeneuve's 126 C at Imola for the Italian Grand Prix in September 1980; it was faster than the boxer 312 T5 but ran in practice only. Above, Villeneuve tries the KKK engine in 126 C 050 during the Friday qualifying session for the 1981 Long Beach Grand Prix. Chassis 049 and 051 were converted from Comprex to KKK engines for the race.

Shown to the press at Fiorano in June 1980, the first 126 C (047) had a 540-bhp KKK-turbocharged 1496-cc V-6, high engine cover and still-legal sliding skirts.

126 C

Engine: *120-degree V-6, mounted ahead of and driving rear wheels. Bore 81 mm, stroke 48.4 mm, displacement 1496.43 cc. Gear-driven twin overhead camshafts for each bank of cylinders, operating two intake and two exhaust valves per cylinder. KKK turbocharger or Comprex supercharger. Ignition by Marelli transistor. Single spark plug per cylinder. Compression ratio 6.5:1. Power output 540-550 bhp at 11,000 rpm. Specific output 360.8-367.5 bhp/liter.*

Transmission: *Dry multi-plate clutch between engine and gearbox. 5 or 6-speed and reverse gearbox mounted transversely behind engine in unit with final drive.*

Chassis: *Monocoque. Fiberglass body panels. Side fairings giving aerodynamic downforce, initially with sliding skirts, later without.*

Suspension: *Front, upper rocker arms, inboard coil spring/shock absorber units, wide-base lower A-arms, anti-roll bar. Rear, universal-jointed halfshafts, upper rocker arms, inboard coil spring/shock absorber units, lower links, anti-roll bar. Lockheed ventilated disc brakes, mounted outboard front and rear. Center-lock Speedline cast magnesium-alloy 13-inch wheels with Michelin radial tires.*

Dimensions: *Wheelbase 2719 mm (107.0 inches). Track 1761 mm (69.3 inches) front, 1626 mm (64.0 inches) rear. Length 4468 mm (175.9 inches). Width 2110 mm (83.1 inches). Height, to rollbar, 1025 mm (40.3 inches). Weight, less fuel and driver, 600 kg (1323 pounds). Weight/power ratio 1.11-10.9 kg (2.44-2.40 pounds)/bhp.*

Note: *Specifications based on 1980 Ferrari press release for original car, plus observed modifications. All figures are potentially variable, especially those for front and rear track and width, dependent on wheels and tires fitted, and weight.*

the "wing" chassis, first by Lotus and then everybody else, made the maximum amount of underbody free space for ground-effect necessary, and although the 312 T4 made a successful compromise between power and handling in 1979, an engine narrower than the boxer was called for. Whether the side pods would be augmented by sliding skirts or not the monocoque had to be slim, and the engine too.

In June 1980, by which time the 312 T5 was having an absolutely miserable season, Ferrari unveiled its all-new car to the press at the factory's Fiorano test track. It was the first 1.5-liter car from Maranello, and the first Formula 1 V-6, since 1965 (not counting the use of the 2.4 Tasman version of the Dino engine in several races in 1966). It was called the 126 C, for 120-degree six, with *compressore* (supercharger), and the selection of this designation, rather than the expected 156 (1.5-liter six), showed an unwillingness to link the car with the earlier Dino, or perhaps a sentimental wish on the part of Enzo Ferrari to relate it to the original Formula 1 Ferrari, the supercharged 125 F1 of 1948-50. Ferrari has always enjoyed playing with numbers, in designations as well as in technology. On the left side the car carried number 1

and Jody Scheckter's name (he was destined to test it briefly, but never race it); on the right number 2 and Gilles Villeneuve's.

As revealed to the press, the first 126 C (chassis 047, falling between the next-to-last and last of the 312 T5 boxers, rather than starting a new series as would have been expected) was a tidy machine, vastly cleaned up in comparison to the T5 but showing some visual similarity. For the first time since 1973 the front wing grew out of the sides of the nose cone rather than being mounted full-width above it; the side pods, employing sliding skirts (still legal in 1980), resembled those of the earlier machines externally but had much improved airflow inside. The cockpit fairing extended well to the back, giving a finned appearance.

Under this fairing (separately removable rather than part of the cockpit cover) sat Forghieri's new baby, a tiny but already potent looking turbocharged engine. With the initial KKK turbo then fitted, the plumbing atop the wide-angle 24-valve V-6 dominated the engine compartment. A figure of 540 bhp at 11,000 rpm was given, with a compression ratio of 6.5:1. Compared to the figure of 515 at 12,300 at 11.5:1 for the T4 and T5, this

D'Alessio cutaway shows the basic components of the 126 C as it appeared for the 1980 Italian Grand Prix. Side-pod ducting is much cleaner than on the 312 T5 boxer.

Villeneuve tests a Comprex-equipped 126 C at Fiorano in the winter of 1981. Engine cover was abbreviated while system was undergoing testing; later cars had longer covers.

was a healthy increase, but the problem of throttle lag plus high stress and heat factors could be expected to limit the turbo's effectiveness at first, as had been Renault's experience. The engine's dimensions were 81 x 48.4 mm, extremely oversquare (again we can compare these to the 80 x 49.6 figures on the 12-cylinder boxer), giving a displacement of 1496 cc. A redesigned version of Ferrari's very successful transverse gearbox and final drive was employed, with five or six speeds.

The suspension employed inboard coil springs operated by rocker arms, front and rear, and the brakes were outboard on all four wheels. The water radiator was located obliquely in the left-hand side pod, near the front, with the oil radiator in the corresponding position on the right and two heat exchangers mounted amidships behind them. A very round figure of 600 kg, equivalent to 1323 pounds, was quoted for the car's total weight; Ferrari has been a bit more realistic in this department than in former years, but the number has to be taken as an approximation, at least until the car is sorted into some form of definitive configuration for the 1980 season.

Changes appeared almost immediately, in testing at Fiorano and at the car's public debut in practice for the Italian Grand Prix at Imola in September. Suspension geometry was revised, the wastegate for the turbocharger was mounted vertically rather than horizontally, the heat exchangers were vertical rather than oblique, and the distinctive high engine cover now sloped down in back, looking more like that on the boxers. At Imola the car (049, the second 126) carried number 2 and was driven enthusiastically by Villeneuve in practice, even though it was not intended that the turbo would race. The performance was partly to keep faith with the Italian fans who were not at all pleased by the T5's dismal record, and partly to give Gilles a chance to relieve his frustrations. The Canadian had been very diplomatic about not criticizing the T5 throughout the season; his hopes for the turbo fortified by 750 miles of testing at Fiorano, must have sustained his morale and he was ready to show what it could do at Imola. What it could do was 1:35.751, six-tenths of a second faster than he achieved with the T5, and he gained the eighth-fastest starting position with that time, even though he used the 312 T5 in the race. It was a promising, if teasing, debut. In comparison, Scheckter, clearly not out to risk anything so near

the end of his driving career, started way back in sixteenth spot in his T5.

Throughout the fall of 1980 and the winter and spring of 1981, while political battles raged between FISA and FOCA for the control of Grand Prix racing, the testing of the 126 C continued at an unrelenting pace. The French driver Didier Pironi joined Villeneuve at Scuderia Ferrari, replacing the departing former World Champion Scheckter. Details were changed all over the car: suspension, brakes (a serious problem with the still overweight car), aerodynamics and most im-

portantly, the engine. While the KKK turbocharger continued to be refined, a completely new type of boost was being developed, the Comprex supercharger produced by Brown, Boveri & Co. of Baden, Switzerland.

The Comprex system uses exhaust energy as does the turbocharger and is engine-driven like the supercharger, but it is not strictly one or the other. Basically, it is an exchanger of pressure waves. A cylindrical rotor consisting of cells arranged axially revolves in a housing that has two end plates, one drawing engine intake air into

Details of the 126 C cars, chassis numbers 049, 050 and 051, which appeared for the first 1981 World Championship race at Long Beach. Chassis 049 and 051 had Comprex-supercharged engines installed and 050 the KKK-turbocharged unit when they turned out for practice on Friday. Cockpit covers for Villeneuve (27) and Pironi (28) were interchangeable. Comprex system can be identified by the short, fat exhaust pipe and long, narrow deflector plate; KKK has two smaller pipes and short, wide deflector plate.

and out of the housing, the other connected to the exhaust flow. As the engine-driven rotor revolves it mixes the high-pressure exhaust gas with the intake air, forcing the air into the combustion chamber at an increased density. The exhaust gas and intake air move back and forth in each cell as the pressure energy is transferred. Brown, Boveri had been testing this system for about 15 years on large engines, entering into a cooperative program with Ferrari in 1979.

By January 1981 the results on the 126 engine were extremely good, providing the same power as with the turbocharger but with a dramatically improved throttle response that pleased both drivers. There was no discernable delay, and Tony Kollbrunner, leader of the Comprex Development Turbomachinery Laboratory, felt that the system would be ideal for the car's racing debut at Long Beach in March; on that circuit instant acceleration was more important than peak power. With the Comprex installed, a smaller wastegate and a simpler exhaust system was seen, characterized by a large, oval-section megaphone-shaped pipe pointing straight out the back. Other

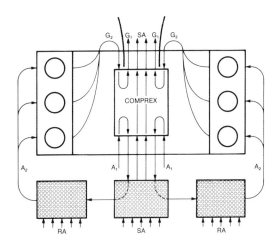

The Comprex, basically designed for passenger-car Diesel engines, is subjected to the extremely severe operating temperatures of a high-speed gasoline engine in the Ferrari Formula 1 racing car. The diagram shows the installation employing the Comprex to deliver compressed charge air A_2 to the engine. The PWS permits the exhaust energy to be used for two purposes: most of this energy (G_2) is used to compress the inlet air A_1. The remainder (G_1) induces charge cooling air flow SA which passes through the rotor and leaves the Comprex with the exhaust gas. In comparison with conventional charge air coolers using ram air RA, this additional cooling air offers the very important advantage that adequate intercooling is available even during stand-still or low vehicle speed.
In the same way as the engine power, this cooling air flow also adjusts instantaneously to load demand.

Overhead views of Villeneuve (27, KKK turbocharger) and Pironi (28, Comprex supercharger) during Friday practice at Long Beach. Note that radiator airfoils are molded into the cockpit cover; rear wings have leading-edge separators.

visible changes included new ducting into the side pods, with the front suspension fairings no longer continuing into the upper surface of the body, which employed sets of three airfoil-shaped vanes at the front of each side pod. These were later eliminated to make a smooth upper surface, with the air exhausting further back, in one experimental version.

The engine cover changed shape according to whether the Comprex or the KKK-equipped engines were installed, and the continued development of the turbocharger was not abandoned. Both Villeneuve and Pironi tested the cars exhaustively at the Fiorano and Paul Richard circuits, the French driver usually with the KKK car. Compared to a best time of 1:08.96 at Fiorano for a 312 T5 with skirts (driven by Pironi for comparison), Villeneuve established a circuit record of 1:08.469 in a skirted 126. The best time there for a skirtless 126 has been Pironi's 1:10.44. At Ricard the best 126 time has been Pironi's 1:05.67, compared to the best time of 1:04.77 by Bruno Giacomelli's Alfa Romeo 179C V-12, so Ferrari still had a way to go before becoming totally competitive. History has shown that Ferrari goes the distance.

During the development period, *Autosprint* magazine has referred to the KKK-equipped car as the 126 K and the Comprex as the 126 C, while a

recent factory release has referred to the latter as the 126 BBC (Brown Boveri Comprex). As the date of the first official World Championship points race at Long Beach approached, the car neared its definitive configuration, with a long engine fairing almost restoring the appearance of the press-debut car nine months before, and new, large "Ferrari" and "FIAT" lettering decorating the flanks. Carrying numbers 27 and 28 (inherited from Williams when that team took over 1 and 2), the cars were shipped to the U.S. Three chassis were prepared: 049 and 051 with Comprex engines and 050 with the KKK. Number 27 for Villeneuve was a Comprex, while two cars, one of each type, carried Pironi's number 28.

In practice on the California circuit the Ferraris were slow to reach competitive times. In the Friday morning unofficial practice session Pironi and Villeneuve were eighth and tenth fastest with times of 1:22.966 and 1:23.224 respectively. At the end of the afternoon qualifying period, after trying both the Comprex and the KKK systems, they had made substantial improvements, Villeneuve moving up to third best with 1:21.723 and Pironi, almost as fast, fifth with 1:21.828. It was current World Champion Alan Jones who set the pace with his Williams FW 07 Cosworth.

On Saturday the Ferrari drivers got their cars around the 2.02-mile course a little quicker, Vil-

Villeneuve's Long Beach race was short, spoiled by a broken driveshaft on lap 17. Pironi fought a long battle in the second group of cars before fuel vaporization slowed and then stopped him. For much of the race he had the best of Piquet's Brabham, Cheever's Tyrrell, Laffite's Ligier-Talbot and Andretti's Alfa Romeo, but he gradually slipped back before retiring.

leneuve with 1:20.462 and Pironi with 1:20.909, but improvements by their competitors (Riccardo Patrese surprising everyone by qualifying the Arrows on the pole) meant that the Ferraris started fifth and eleventh. In comparison to the howl of the old flat-12 engines, the Comprex-equipped V-6 Ferraris had a much subdued, whistling sound, while the KKK cars were characterized by a deep, firecracker-like backfire on the overrun; it was now the Alfa Romeo and Matra V-12s which provided the most audible exhaust notes.

Surprisingly, considering the reduced throttle lag of the Comprex, Ferrari had better hopes for the KKK-equipped engines, both of the starting cars (049 and 051) using turbos. In the race Villeneuve and Pironi made good use of their speed on Shoreline Drive, coming around in 4th and 6th positions, sandwiching Nelson Piquet's Brabham, on the first lap. The order of this trio was reversed when Villeneuve braked late for the Queen's Hairpin and overshot, Pironi passing both him and Piquet.

Patrese and the two Williams cars of Carlos Reutemann and Jones were already moving away up front; in the next group the order was Pironi, Piquet, Villeneuve, Eddie Cheever's Tyrrell and Mario Andretti's Alfa Romeo. Villeneuve's 126 C was missing on lap 18, suffering a broken drive-shaft, but Pironi kept the other car ahead of Piquet for many laps until fuel vaporization started to affect his engine. First Piquet, next Cheever and then Andretti passed Pironi, the Alfa staying ahead only after a long battle during which the straightaway speed of the 126 C was sufficient to make up for the time lost on the tighter parts of the circuit. This duel between two Italian cars was probably the most exciting aspect of the Long Beach race.

Out in front, Jones ultimately won after Patrese retired and Reutemann slowed. Pironi's fuel problem finally caused his retirement after 66 laps, at which point he was in 10th position but not classified as a finisher, not having gone 90 percent of race distance. He had driven an excellent debut race for Ferrari. The two 126 C cars had shown real speed and the retirements were not unexpected for a brand new design.

On the other hand, the cars were definitely overweight at an estimated 610 kg (1345 pounds), compounding the problems of braking and acceleration, and the handling was clearly not in the same class with that of the Williams. But Long Beach is the least suitable circuit for a turbocharged engine (the turbo Renaults were much further back and never in contention) and a lightened 126 C with a fully developed Comprex boost can be competitive on the other circuits in 1981.

Ghia *bodywork on Ferrari chassis*

THE EARLIEST FERRARI road cars were built with *carrozzeria* by Touring and then Vignale, before the majority of production was taken over by Pininfarina in the mid 1950s. But a number of chassis, probably at least 32 and perhaps as many as 35, were built with bodywork by Carrozzeria Ghia SpA, Torino.

Most of them, on 166 Inter, 195 Inter, 212 Inter and 340 America chassis, were relatively sedate, with handsome if not exciting lines. There were two basic body styles, a fairly crisp berlinetta and a taller and much less appealing four-passenger coupe (actually called a *berlina*, or sedan, by Ghia themselves). The earliest 166 and 195 berlinettas had a slight recess between the front fenders and the relatively high hood; this did not maintain the by-then already traditional oval Ferrari grille shape but it had the advantage of giving the car a much lighter appearance overall. When the same basic design, conceived by Mario Felice Boano while he was head of Ghia styling during 1948-53, was adapted to the 212 chassis it received a simpler but heavier-look-hoodline. And it was also stretched to fit several 340 America chassis; on these the rear "fender" forms were extended forward to balance the longer front fenders but the result was awkward.

With their restrained character and fully appointed interiors, the Ghia Ferraris were about as far away from competition machinery as was possible on a Maranello product, but several of them *were* raced. The only one to do anything

significant in this area was Tony Parravano's 340 American berlinetta (0150 A). Bill Pollack drove the unwieldy car without success at Torrey Pines in 1952; in the Carrera Panamericana that year Jack McAfee and Ernie McAfee (no relation) drove the same car, extensively modified by the latter and including Halibrand disc wheels, to an excellent 5th place overall. With 4.1 liters and the expertise of the two McAfees, even this heavy car was fast. It was a Ferrari, after all.

Another variation on Boano's basic shape, a very nice notch-back coupe was built over a 212 Inter chassis (0213 EL). But the remainder of the Ghia Ferraris, especially the last few from the firm's declining years, were not well designed. The 212 Europa shown at Paris in 1952 was a bulky two-tone car with some of the Exner influence from the Chrysler association, and perhaps a hint of Karmann Ghia VW styling to come. At least two cabriolets were built on 212 Inter chassis.

The last two Ghia Ferraris were a 375 America coupe (0347 AL) and a 410 Superamerica coupe (0473 SA). The former was over-detailed and sported an excessive two-tone (and later three-tone) paint scheme, apparently salmon and black (this latter color possibly navy blue). The 410 SA, built for Bob Wilke, adapted the tailfin theme of Ghia's Gilda and Dart to the biggest Ferrari chassis in 1956. The overall shape was dramatic but huge, with an extremely clumsy front end—not the best finish for a basically rewarding relationship between manufacturer and body builder.

Boano-designed Ghia berlinetta body on 166 Inter chassis was well proportioned and well detailed, although grille shape, with center raised for hood height, was not the regular Ferrari oval. Interior was simple but handsome.

Variation on 166 style was used on a number of 195 Inters. Contours were essentially the same, with different details from car to car. Ghia building is in the background.

38

Ghia berlinetta style underwent significant changes for 212 Inter; grille was now the Ferrari oval, making the nose heavier-looking, and quarter windows were rounded.

Owner with 212 Inter only **looks** *like Enzo Ferrari. Cabriolet style, of which two were built, was not as handsome as berlinettas.*

Berlina 4 posti style on 212 Inter chassis was staid but nicely detailed.

Clipping from race program shows Ghia 212 Berlina handling most ungracefully in U.S. event.

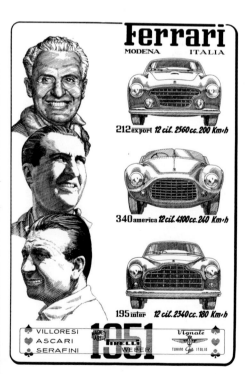

Ferrari ad in Motor Italia *showed drawing of Ghia-bodied 195 Inter berlinetta along with Vignale 212 berlinetta and Touring 340 America barchetta.*

Ghia Ferraris

1	*166 Inter Berlinetta 2 posti. Serial number 049 S; possibly others.*
10	*195 Inter Berlinetta 2 posti. Serial numbers 0059 S, 0087 S, 0089 S, 0093 S, 0101 S, 0109 S, 0113 S, 0121 S, 0129 S, 0133 S. Examples shown at Geneva and Torino 1951.*
8	*212 Inter Berlinetta 2 posti. Serial numbers 0105 S, 0149 E, 0153 E, 0155 E, 0169 E, 0183 EL, 0185 EL, 0189 E. Example shown at Torino 1952.*
2	*212 Inter Berlina 4 posti. Serial numbers 0193 EL, 0199 EL.*
2	*212 Inter Cabriolet 2 posti. Serial number 0191 E; other unknown. Shown at Torino 1952.*

1	*212 Inter Coupe 2 posti. Serial number 0213 EL.*
1	*212 Europa Coupe Sport 2 posti. Serial number unknown. Shown at Paris 1952.*
2	*340 America Berlina 4 posti. Serial number 0130 AL; at least one other, possibly several. Shown at Paris 1951.*
5	*340 America Berlinetta 2 posti. Serial numbers 0142 A, 0148 A, 0150 A; probably two others.*
1	*375 America Coupe 2 posti. Serial number 0347 AL. Shown at Torino 1955.*
1	*410 Superamerica Coupe Sport 2 posti. Serial number 0473 SA.*

34 cars; probable range 32-35 examples.

212 Inter Coupe 2 posti (0213 EL) was a very attractive variation on the berlinetta form. Two-tone looks good here.

Showing influence of Exner designs built for Chrysler, 212 Europa Coupe Sport was massive in appearance. Car was shown at 1952 Paris Salon.

340 America Berlina body was almost identical to that on 212 Inter, except for thin rub strip on each flank.

John Perona was one of at least three customers for Ghia's 340 America berlinettas. Note the substitution of American bumpers. Car is seen in company with Cunningham C4RK at Sebring.

Parravano's 340 America was initially identical to Perona's but was significantly modified by Ernie McAfee, driven by him and Jack McAfee to an excellent 5th place in Mexico.

Neither the design sketch nor the final result was very successful on this one-of-a-kind 375 America Coupe 2 posti shown at Torino in 1955. Interior looks almost American, except for the steering wheel and gear lever.

42

FERRARI 410 *America*

*410 Superamerica Coupe Sport
2 posti built for Bob Wilke
was a huge Ferrari variation on
Ghia's Gilda and Dart designs.
Construction shot emphasizes
the car's great bulk.*

43

Bob Tronolone Portfolio

Front-engine Ferrari sports cars in California races

BOB TRONOLONE *was born in New York City in 1935 but grew up in Tucson, where he received a Bachelor of Science degree from the University of Arizona in 1958. Since then he has lived in California, where he works for Hughes Aircraft Co. His first camera was a 35mm Canon rangefinder which he bought while serving with the U.S. Army in Korea in 1956 and the first race he photographed was a USAC stock car event at the Arizona State Fairgrounds in Phoenix in 1957.*

From then on he has shot nearly every important road racing event in California, from the amateur Cal Club sports car races through Can-Am to Formula 1, as well as USAC and CART competition in California and Arizona and including an annual trek to Indianapolis, which he has covered every year since 1961.

A charter member of the American Racing Press Association and a contributing photographer to Road & Track *magazine, Bob now uses Nikon equipment, with Nikkor lenses ranging from 28 to 500mm. While he feels that the most spectacular form of competition to photograph is "Big Car" one-mile dirt-oval racing, he has most enjoyed the Cal Club weekends of the late 1950s and SCCA Can-Am events of the late 1960s. His favorite driver currently racing is Mario Andretti.*

In addition to the technical proficiency his work has shown, Bob's coverage has been notable for the different camera angles he has used, especially the downward shots at Laguna Seca and Long Beach, taken from trees and condemned buildings!

This selection of photos taken at sports car races during 1958-60 is not representative of his current work (see the 126 C coverage from Long Beach on pages 32-35) but was chosen for the appeal of the front-engine Ferraris racing then, some of them familiar, some not so well-known.

Richie Ginther in John von Neumann's 250 TR (0710) at Laguna Seca in 1958.
Josie von Neumann drives the same pontoon-fendered car at Hourglass Field, San Diego, in 1959.

A fine profile shot of Ginther in Von Neumann's other 250 TR (0704) at Hourglass Field in 1959.

Tachometer shot shows rev limit at 6500 rpm, telltale at 8000.

Three-liter TR engine had six Weber 38 DCN carburetors.

Pedro Rodriguez in number 5 (0718) in the Kiwanis Grand Prix at Riverside in 1959.

Dick Morgensen in his pontoon-fender 250 TR number 46 (0756) at Del Mar the same year.

Von Neumann's Competition Motors lineup at Riverside in July 1959. Number 112 (with Josie Von Neumann) is the 250 TR (0704), 211 is Ginther's 412 MI (0744) and 5 is Rodriguez' 250 TR (0718). In the background, its door open, is Jack Nethercutt's 500 TRC, number 102.

47

Ginther in the 412 MI at Riverside in October 1959, leading Hill's 250 TR 59 (0768) in the Times GP.

Ken Miles in the ex-Parravano 121 LM at Santa Barbara in 1958.

An early-morning paddock scene at Laguna Seca 1958; in the foreground, the Von Neumann 250 TR of Richie Ginther (0704).

Hill's 250 TR 59 leads Bob Oker in the big 410 Sport and Ken Miles in a Porsche in the 1959 Times GP. In the lower photo he is sandwiched between Oker and Morgensen's 250 TR.

50

Jack Nethercutt bought 0768 from Von Neumann and raced it in 1960-61. The pit shot (Pomona SCCA Regional, 1960) shows the immaculate finish, while the competition shot (Hanford 1960) gives a good rear view as it enters the banking.

Two big guns at Riverside in 1958. Joakim Bonnier was one of many drivers of the 4.9-liter
410 Sport, the Edgar car, used only once by the factory at Buenos Aires in 1956. John von Neumann
drives his 4-cam, 4.1-liter 335 S past the same spot; its nose resembles that of his first 250 TR (0710).

The 500 TRC was one of the most beautiful Ferraris ever made and the superb finish of Nethercutt's all-red car, seen at the Cal Club Regional race at Santa Barbara in 1959, doesn't hurt a bit. A fairly rare type was the Touring-bodied 340 MM, raced by Nino Farina, Mike Hawthorn and Hans Ruesch in Europe; in this photo, handling it at Santa Barbara in 1959, is Jack Brumby.

Troy Ruttman (number 38) and Rodger Ward (163) were among several drivers given the unenviable task of racing the ex-Parravano 121 LM during its last years. These shots from 1959 were taken at Pomona and Riverside in July and October, respectively

Another ex-Parravano car, a 750 Monza, smokes at Del Mar in 1959.

Is it still a Ferrari with a Chevy in it? Bill Love tries V-8 power in this 500 Mondial in Pomona 6-hour race in 1958.

Ferrari BB 512 LM,
308 GTB/4 Turbo and
365 GTB/4 run at Daytona

FERRARI DID NOT achieve much in the way of concrete results at Daytona in 1981, but Maranello machinery provided variety, drama and impressive speed. One each 365 GTB/4, BB 512 LM and 308 GTB 4 Turbo were entered. The front-engine Daytona, named for the Florida circuit after the 1967 victory by a trio of 330 P4s, is almost a historic vehicle by now, with a long career that includes a 2nd place in the 1979 event. The 1981 entry, made by Crevier Imports for Joe Crevier/Pete Halsmer/Al Unser Jr., qualified 46th out of a field of 72 cars with a time of 2:06.344; it started to burn when a fuel line fractured on lap 11 with Unser at the wheel and left the circuit in flames.

Qualifying a respectable 24th at 1:57.664, the Prancing Horse Farm BB 512 LM/80 (Paul Pappalardo's 32131) of Tony Adamowicz/Rick Knoop was running a strong 3rd when it was involved in the crash of Giampiero Moretti's Porsche 935 on lap 529 and forced out with exten-

sive damage. This was the most competitive Berlinetta Boxer yet seen, prepared by Lee Dykstra with special BBS wheels, 16-inch front and 19 rear, to accommodate a proper set of Lockheed brakes. Tested by Al Holbert and John Paul, it set a BB lap record at Fiorano.

The shortest but most impressive performance was that of the Jolly Club 308 GTB 4 Turbo of Carlo Facetti/Martino Finotto, who qualified it 7th quickest at 1:46.914 and set the fastest race lap in 1:48.14 (205.568 km/h) on its third tour; unfortunately it lasted just one more lap before the water radiator burst. The 32-valve Garrett twin-turbocharged 308 engine has shown 833 bhp on the test stand, and the Group 5 car, under development by Facetti for several years, must represent the most serious attempt to field a race-winning prototype Ferrari since the factory retired its 312 PBs at the end of 1973. The 308 GTB 4 Turbo may be a real threat in the shorter races.

1981

Opposite page, the Prancing Horse Farm BB 512 LM which was running 3rd when involved in a crash. Above, Carlo Facetti's 308 GTB 4 Turbo, which set the lap record just before retiring with water radiator failure. Below, the 365 GTBs4 Daytona entered by Crevier; it caught fire on lap 9 and retired on lap 11.

Ferrari Victories
at the Nürburgring

20 August 1950	German GP	Alberto Ascari	166 F2
29 July 1951	German GP	Alberto Ascari	375 F1
25 May 1952	Eifelrennen	Rudi Fischer	500 F2
3 August 1952	German GP	Alberto Ascari	500 F2
2 August 1953	German GP	Nino Farina	500 F2
30 August 1953	1000-km Race	Alberto Ascari/Nino Farina	375 MM
5 August 1956	German GP	Juan Manuel Fangio	D50 F1
27 May 1962	1000-km Race	Phil Hill/Olivier Gendebien	246 SP
19 May 1963	1000-km Race	John Surtees/Willy Mairesse	250 P
4 August 1963	German GP	John Surtees	156 F1
31 May 1964	1000-km Race	Lodovico Scarfiotti/Nino Vaccarella	275 P
2 August 1964	German GP	John Surtees	158 F1
23 May 1965	1000-km Race	John Surtees/Lodovico Scarfiotti	330 P2
28 May 1972	1000-km Race	Ronnie Peterson/Tim Schenken	312 PB
30 July 1972	German GP	Jacky Ickx	312 B2
27 May 1973	1000-km Race	Jacky Ickx/Brian Redman	312 PB
4 August 1974	German GP	Clay Regazzoni	312 B3

Ferrari also won the Gran Turismo category in the 1000-km race in the following years:

1958	"Beurlys" (Jean Blaton)/Leon Dernier	250 GT LWB
1959	"Beurlys"/"Blary" (A. Blaton)	250 GT LWB
1960	Carlo Maria Abate/Colin Davis	250 GT LWB
1961	Carlo Maria Abate/Colin Davis	250 GT SWB
1962	Wolfgang Seidel/Nocker	250 GT SWB
1963	Pierre Noblet/Jean Guichet	250 GTO
1964	Mike Parkes/Jean Guichet	250 GTO 64

THE NÜRBURGRING, a 22.81-km road course built in the Eifel mountains of western Germany especially for racing in the late 1920s, is a legendary circuit that has seen everything from the huge supercharged Mercedes-Benz and Auto Union Grand Prix cars of 1934-39 to Touring Car endurance racing with BMW 700s and Fiat-Abarths. It has always challenged the skills of the most brilliant drivers from Tazio Nuvolari through Niki Lauda, but has not been used for Formula 1 events since the latter's near-fatal crash there in 1976.

Scuderia Ferrari raced its Alfa Romeos at the Nürburgring in the 1930s and between 1950 and 1976 was represented in every important international event on the Eifel circuit. The major races each year were the Nürburgring 1000-Km Rennen

58

Nürburgring

for sports cars in late May and the Grosser Preis von Deutschland for Grand Prix cars in early August, both events counting toward their respective world championships. Ferrari was a consistent winner at the Nürburgring in both categories, even in years when the Scuderia was not especially competitive on other circuits. But the reverse was sometimes true, Maserati and Aston Martin doing extremely well there from 1956 through 1961 and Lotus defeating the otherwise dominant Dino 156 F1 in 1961. It was usually Stirling Moss who thwarted Ferrari hopes at the Ring!

Of the sixteen championship victories scored by Ferrari in the Eifel mountains (nine in Formula 1 and seven in sports car events), Alberto Ascari and John Surtees each scored four. Jacky Ickx,

perhaps the most brilliant Ring driver of all, won twice for Ferrari, as did Nino Farina and Lodovico Scarfiotti. The accompanying list of Maranello victories, impressive as it is, only scratches the surfaces of the team's performances there, with frequent 2nd place when victory was not possible, and many lap records, including the first qualifying lap under nine minutes (Phil Hill, 8:55.2, 1961) and the first under seven (Lauda, 6:58.6, 1975).

This pictorial shows the rich variety of Ferraris that ran at the Nürburgring over a period of nearly thirty years, including Formula 1, Formula 2, sports/racing and Gran Turismo machinery, as well as road cars only mildly prepared for competition by their private owners.

Among the Alfa Romeos raced by Scuderia Ferrari at the Nürburgring before World War 2 were the 12C 36 Grand Prix cars; at the wheel in these photos are the great Tazio Nuvolari (number 22) and Nino Farina (12).

Right, Niki Lauda's 312T leads the field at the start of the 1975 German Grand Prix; he was 3rd after stopping to replace a tire. Below, the 312 PB of Jacky Ickx and Brian Redman, who won the 1973 1000-km race. Opposite page, top, Clay Regazzoni takes to the air in his 312 B3, on the way to winning the 1974 Grand Prix. Opposite page, bottom, Scuderia Ferrari mechanics warm up the 801 F1 T-car before the start of practice for the 1957 Grand Prix.

60

1950: Mme. Yvonne Simon, 166 MM Touring berlinetta.

1950: Alberto Ascari, 166 F2.

1950: *Dorino Serafini (4) and Alberto Ascari (2), 166 F2.*

64

1951: Luigi Villoresi's 375 F1.

1952: Alberto Ascari (101) and Nino Farina (102), 500 F2.

1952: Rudi Fischer, 500 F2.

1952: Jacques Peron, 212 Export Vignale berlinetta.

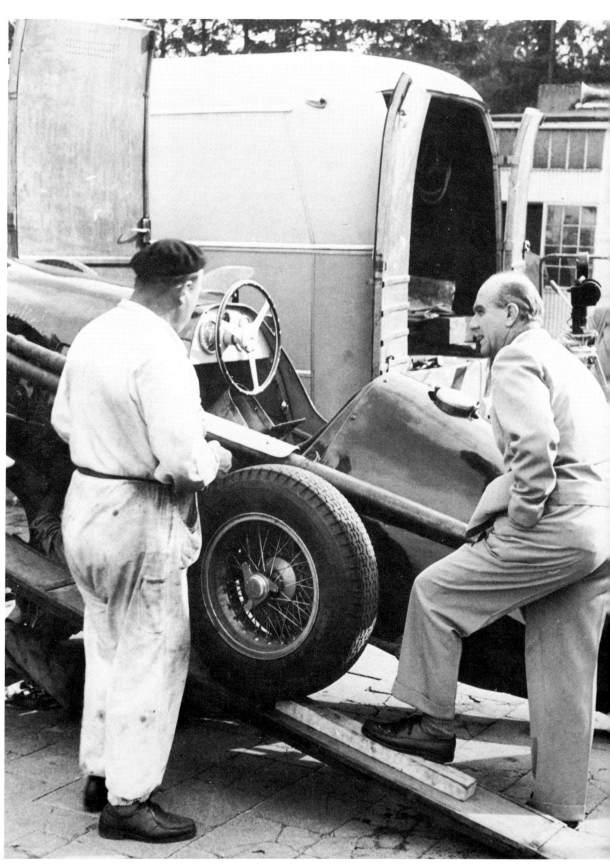

1953: Nino Farina, 500 F2.

1953: Alberto Ascari/Nino Farina, 375 MM Vignale spyder.

1953: Kurt Zeller, 500 Mondial Pinin Farina berlinetta.

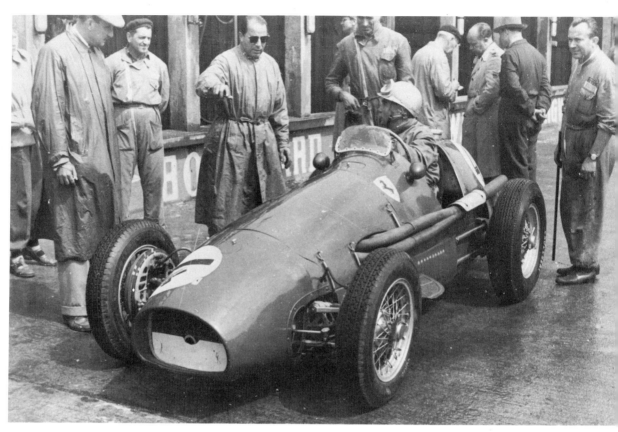

1954: Piero Taruffi, 625 F1.

1955: Willy Daetwyler, 750 Monza.

1956: Luigi Musso (3), 290 MM; Eugenio Castellotti (2), 860 Monza; Juan Manuel Fangio (1), 860 Monza; Phil Hill (4), 290 MM.

69

1956: Juan Manuel Fangio (1), Peter Collins (2), Eugenio Castellotti (3) and Luigi Musso (4); Lancia D50 F1

1957: Olivier Gendebien, 335 S.

1957: Masten Gregory, 250 TR prototype.

1957: Wolfgang Seidel, 250 GT Pinin Farina LWB berlinetta.

1957: Luigi Musso, Peter Collins and Mike Hawthorn's 801 F1 (6, 7, 8).

1958: Phil Hill, 250 TR.

1958: Peter Collins, Dino 246 F1.

1958: Phil Hill, Dino 156 F2.

*1959: "Beurlys" (Jean Blaton),
250 GT Pinin Farina LWB beriinetta.*

1959: Jean Behra (3) and Phil Hill (4), 250 TR 59.

1960: Phil Hill, 250 TRI 60.

1960: Giorgio Scarlatti's Dino 246 S.

1961: Pedro Rodriguez, 250 TR 60/61.

Karussell

KOLBEN-KRÄMER KÖLN

KOLBEN·ZYLNDER·KURBELWELLEN·LAGER

1961: Phil Hill, Dino 156 F1.

78

1962: Ricardo Rodriguez' Dino 156 F1.

1962: Mike Parkes, 250 GTO 4-liter.

1963: John Surtees (110) and Lodovico Scarfiotti (111), 250 P; Karl von Czazy (48), 250 GTO.

1963: Jean Guichet, 250 GTO.

1963: John Surtees, Dino 156 F1.

1964: Mike Parkes (83), 250 GTO 64; Manfred Ramminger (76), 250 GTO.

1964: John Surtees (143), 275 P, and Jochen Rindt (134), 250 LM.

1964: John Surtees, 158 Fl.

1964: Lorenzo Bandini, Dino 156 Fl.

84

1965: Willy Mairesse (5), 250 LM, and Lorenzo Bandini (31), Dino 166 P.

1965: John Surtees, 330 P2

1965: Giancarlo Baghetti/Giampiero Biscaldi's 275 GTB/C.

1966: Mike Parkes, 330 P3 spyder.

1966: Lorenzo Bandini, 312 F1.

1967: Jean Guichet, Dino 206 SP.

88

1967: Chris Amon, 312 F1.

1968: Jacky Ickx, 312 F1.

90

1970: Herbert Müller, 512 S berlinetta.

1971: Jacky Ickx, 312 B2 F1.

1972: Jacky Ickx, 312 B2 F1.

1972: Ronnie Peterson, 312 PB.

1973: Arturo Merzario, 312 PB.

94

1975: Niki Lauda, 312 T.

1976: Niki Lauda, 312 T2.

ISBN 0-940014-01-7

Acknowledgements

Photographs by Vicente Alvarez, Dean Batchelor, Pete Coltrin, Art Flores, Geoffrey Goddard, Thom Henkel, Italfoto, Corrado Millanta, Kurt Miska, Günther Molter, Phipps Photographic, Publifoto, Rainer Schlegelmilch, Jim Sitz, Bob Tronolone and Kurt Wörner.

In addition, the editor would like to thank Ernie Beutler, SpA Ferrari SEFAC, Ferrari North America, Paul Harsanyi, Michael Lynch, Jean-Francois Marchet, Bill Oursler, Paul Pappalardo, Chuck Queener and Gerald Roush for the material and assistance which they generously provided.

96 FERRARI ALBUM is a continuing publication. We welcome any comments, additions or corrections which readers may be able to provide, as well as original material for future publication. Please address all editorial correspondence to Jonathan Thompson, P.O. Box 618, Norwell, Massachusetts 02061.

FERRARI ALBUM is published approximately four times a year. Readers wishing to be kept up to date on the details and publication announcements of forthcoming editions should write directly to Ferrari Album, The Color Market, 3000 Dundee Road, Suite 201, Northbrook, Illinois 60062.